Hello Awesome!

You are fucking amazing.

And this planner will help you enjoy the kickass year that you deserve.

The *I Swear Because I Care Planner* is filled with funny motivational quotes, calendars and checklists that will brighten the fuck out of your day and help you crush your goals.

Are you ready to say?

✓ Fuck YES! to...	✗ Fuck NO! to...
Loving the fuck out of yourself	Being a bitch to yourself
Saving your fucks for important shit	Assholes and bullshit
Getting shit done	Shitshows and overwhelm
Laughing your ass off	Boring affirmations

Okay then, you beautiful, uncensored, unstoppable badass!

Let's fucking go!

I Swear Because I Care 2025 Planner. Funny Motivational Organizer With Over 100 Sweary Affirmations and Quotations

Sassy Quotes Press

Helping badass women laugh and get shit done since 2021

Copyright ©2024. All rights reserved. SASSYQUOTESPRESS.COM

ISBN: 978-1-957633-50-3

Questions? Comments?

I would love to hear from you! Please email Jen@SassyQuotesPress.com

Ready for your fabulous Bonus Gifts?

Go to the **Bonus Gifts** page at the back of this book for instant access download info.

Bonus Gift Printables

48 Sweary Affirmation Cards
Funny Wall Art Posters
Swear Word Coloring Pages

Sign up for more freebies and updates at SASSYQUOTESPRESS.COM

2025

JANUARY

S	M	T	W	T	F	S
			1	2	3	4
5	6	7	8	9	10	11
12	13	14	15	16	17	18
19	20	21	22	23	24	25
26	27	28	29	30	31	

FEBRUARY

S	M	T	W	T	F	S
						1
2	3	4	5	6	7	8
9	10	11	12	13	14	15
16	17	18	19	20	21	22
23	24	25	26	27	28	

MARCH

S	M	T	W	T	F	S
						1
2	3	4	5	6	7	8
9	10	11	12	13	14	15
16	17	18	19	20	21	22
23	24	25	26	27	28	29
30	31					

APRIL

S	M	T	W	T	F	S
		1	2	3	4	5
6	7	8	9	10	11	12
13	14	15	16	17	18	19
20	21	22	23	24	25	26
27	28	29	30			

MAY

S	M	T	W	T	F	S
				1	2	3
4	5	6	7	8	9	10
11	12	13	14	15	16	17
18	19	20	21	22	23	24
25	26	27	28	29	30	31

JUNE

S	M	T	W	T	F	S
1	2	3	4	5	6	7
8	9	10	11	12	13	14
15	16	17	18	19	20	21
22	23	24	25	26	27	28
29	30					

JULY

S	M	T	W	T	F	S
		1	2	3	4	5
6	7	8	9	10	11	12
13	14	15	16	17	18	19
20	21	22	23	24	25	26
27	28	29	30	31		

AUGUST

S	M	T	W	T	F	S
					1	2
3	4	5	6	7	8	9
10	11	12	13	14	15	16
17	18	19	20	21	22	23
24	25	26	27	28	29	30
31						

SEPTEMBER

S	M	T	W	T	F	S
	1	2	3	4	5	6
7	8	9	10	11	12	13
14	15	16	17	18	19	20
21	22	23	24	25	26	27
28	29	30				

OCTOBER

S	M	T	W	T	F	S
			1	2	3	4
5	6	7	8	9	10	11
12	13	14	15	16	17	18
19	20	21	22	23	24	25
26	27	28	29	30	31	

NOVEMBER

S	M	T	W	T	F	S
						1
2	3	4	5	6	7	8
9	10	11	12	13	14	15
16	17	18	19	20	21	22
23	24	25	26	27	28	29
30						

DECEMBER

S	M	T	W	T	F	S
	1	2	3	4	5	6
7	8	9	10	11	12	13
14	15	16	17	18	19	20
21	22	23	24	25	26	27
28	29	30	31			

2026

JANUARY
S	M	T	W	T	F	S
				1	2	3
4	5	6	7	8	9	10
11	12	13	14	15	16	17
18	19	20	21	22	23	24
25	26	27	28	29	30	31

FEBRUARY
S	M	T	W	T	F	S
1	2	3	4	5	6	7
8	9	10	11	12	13	14
15	16	17	18	19	20	21
22	23	24	25	26	27	28

MARCH
S	M	T	W	T	F	S
1	2	3	4	5	6	7
8	9	10	11	12	13	14
15	16	17	18	19	20	21
22	23	24	25	26	27	28
29	30	31				

APRIL
S	M	T	W	T	F	S
			1	2	3	4
5	6	7	8	9	10	11
12	13	14	15	16	17	18
19	20	21	22	23	24	25
26	27	28	29	30		

MAY
S	M	T	W	T	F	S
					1	2
3	4	5	6	7	8	9
10	11	12	13	14	15	16
17	18	19	20	21	22	23
24	25	26	27	28	29	30
31						

JUNE
S	M	T	W	T	F	S
	1	2	3	4	5	6
7	8	9	10	11	12	13
14	15	16	17	18	19	20
21	22	23	24	25	26	27
28	29	30				

JULY
S	M	T	W	T	F	S
			1	2	3	4
5	6	7	8	9	10	11
12	13	14	15	16	17	18
19	20	21	22	23	24	25
26	27	28	29	30	31	

AUGUST
S	M	T	W	T	F	S
						1
2	3	4	5	6	7	8
9	10	11	12	13	14	15
16	17	18	19	20	21	22
23	24	25	26	27	28	29
30	31					

SEPTEMBER
S	M	T	W	T	F	S
		1	2	3	4	5
6	7	8	9	10	11	12
13	14	15	16	17	18	19
20	21	22	23	24	25	26
27	28	29	30			

OCTOBER
S	M	T	W	T	F	S
				1	2	3
4	5	6	7	8	9	10
11	12	13	14	15	16	17
18	19	20	21	22	23	24
25	26	27	28	29	30	31

NOVEMBER
S	M	T	W	T	F	S
1	2	3	4	5	6	7
8	9	10	11	12	13	14
15	16	17	18	19	20	21
22	23	24	25	26	27	28
29	30					

DECEMBER
S	M	T	W	T	F	S
		1	2	3	4	5
6	7	8	9	10	11	12
13	14	15	16	17	18	19
20	21	22	23	24	25	26
27	28	29	30	31		

✓ Fuck YES! Goals & Shit

What goals do you want to crush with your awesomeness? Self care, relationships, hobbies, work? Your possibilities are endless.

_____
_____
_____
_____
_____
_____
_____
_____
_____
_____
_____
_____
_____
_____
_____
_____
_____
_____
_____
_____

☒ Fuck NO! Bullshit

The best way to let more happiness into your life is to get rid of soul-sucking fuckery. Toxic people, negative thoughts, perfectionism and other shit can fuck off! What bullshit will you trash?

_____
_____
_____
_____
_____
_____
_____
_____
_____
_____
_____
_____
_____
_____
_____
_____
_____
_____
_____

☒ Fuck NO! Assholes

You can do hard things, but putting up with assholes shouldn't be one of them! With this handy list of insults and comebacks, you'll always have a creative way to say "Fuck off!"

1. You're about as useful as shit-scented deodorant.
2. I wouldn't say that you're a huge asshole, but YOUR anus is also bigger than Pluto.
3. I don't wish you were dead. I just think your breathing is excessive.
4. You're not "butt ugly," but your face does make penises look good.
5. You're so full of shit, your doorbell says "ding dung."
6. That's cute. You think you're the personality hire, but we know you're the dumpster fire.
7. Check your phone. I think you forgot to take it off Asshole Mode.
8. I wouldn't say you're an idiot, but your brain does identify as a rock.
9. To the world, you are an asshole. But to me, you are also an asshole.
10. "WTF!?," you ask? Your guess is as good as mine, but your ass is not.
11. Annoying the shit out of people is NOT a love language.
12. I'm trying to understand what you're saying, but Google translate is just giving me fart sounds.
13. You are what you eat, and you're clearly a poop-ivore.
14. Being a huge asshole and people liking you is not a thing.
15. I'm not gaslighting you. I think you're just breathing your own farts.
16. You're so dumb, you shouldn't even be allowed to own finger guns.
17. I hate to disappoint you, but... oh wait, it's actually quite nice.
18. I'm done practicing gratitude. I'm so fucking grateful that I'm not you, I've gone pro.
19. You're the whole package: a total dick.
20. Let's play a fun game of "Hide-and-Go-Fuck-Yourself."
21. They say that absence makes the heart grow fonder, so we'd love it if you'd go the fuck away.
22. I wouldn't say you're a dumbass. But wisdom-free is fair.
23. At least there's a method to your madness. Fuck up, rinse, repeat.
24. It doesn't take a rocket scientist to wish you were living on Mars.
25. With all due respect, fuck you.

2025 Plan

- ☑ **LIVE** your badass life
- ☑ **LAUGH** your ass off
- ☑ **LOVE** the fuck out of yourself

let's fucking go!

December-January 2025

30 Monday

31 Tuesday
New Year's Eve

1 Wednesday
New Year's Day

Important as fuck

Fucking grateful for…

New year, same Fuck It era!

2 Thursday

3 Friday

4 Saturday

5 Sunday

Notes and shit

January 2025

Sunday	Monday	Tuesday	Wednesday
DECEMBER 2024 S M T W T F S 1 2 3 4 5 6 7 8 9 10 11 12 13 14 15 16 17 18 19 20 21 22 23 24 25 26 27 28 29 30 31	**FEBRUARY 2025** S M T W T F S 1 2 3 4 5 6 7 8 9 10 11 12 13 14 15 16 17 18 19 20 21 22 23 24 25 26 27 28		1 New Year's Day
5	6	7	8
12	13	14	15
19	20 Martin Luther King Jr. Day (US), Inauguration Day (US)	21	22
26	27 Australia Day (AU)	28	29 Chinese New Year

You pay your fucking dues. So own your fucking awesomeness.

Thursday	Friday	Saturday	Important shit
2	3	4	_____
9	10	11	_____
16	17	18	_____
23	24	25	_____
30	31		_____

January 2025

6 Monday

7 Tuesday

8 Wednesday

Important as fuck

Fucking grateful for...

Ka-POW, bitch! Time to bring that badass energy.

9 Thursday

10 Friday

11 Saturday

-
-
-

12 Sunday

-
-
-

Notes and shit

January 2025

13 Monday   14 Tuesday   15 Wednesday

Important as fuck

Fucking grateful for…

You are a fucking star. But keep reaching for the stars anyway. Because you're not a lazy star. #fuckingstargoals

16 Thursday

17 Friday

18 Saturday

19 Sunday

Notes and shit

January 2025

20 Monday
Martin Luther King Jr. Day (US),
Inauguration Day (US)

21 Tuesday

22 Wednesday

Important as fuck

Fucking grateful for...

Take a deep breath, check your nails, and make shit happen

23 Thursday

24 Friday

25 Saturday

26 Sunday

Notes and shit

January-February 2025

27 Monday
Australia Day (AU)

28 Tuesday

29 Wednesday
Chinese New Year

Important as fuck

Fucking grateful for…

Your eyes sparkle with wisdom, curiosity, and mischief. What the fuck are you up to, bitch?

30 Thursday

31 Friday

1 Saturday

2 Sunday
Groundhog Day (US, CA)

Notes and shit

February 2025

Sunday	Monday	Tuesday	Wednesday
JANUARY 2025 S M T W T F S 　　　 1 2 3 4 5 6 7 8 9 10 11 12 13 14 15 16 17 18 19 20 21 22 23 24 25 26 27 28 29 30 31	**MARCH 2025** S M T W T F S 　　　　　　 1 2 3 4 5 6 7 8 9 10 11 12 13 14 15 16 17 18 19 20 21 22 23 24 25 26 27 28 29 30 31		
2 Groundhog Day (US, CA)	3	4	5
9	10	11	12
16	17 Presidents' Day (US)	18	19
23	24	25	26

You are even stronger than your fucking language

Thursday	Friday	Saturday	Important shit
		1	_____
6	7	8	_____
13	14 Valentine's Day	15	_____
20	21	22	_____
27	28 Ramadan begins		_____

February 2025

3 Monday

4 Tuesday

5 Wednesday

Important as fuck

Fucking grateful for...

If swear words are "colorful language," maybe add "Fucking Artist" to your profiles?

6 Thursday

7 Friday

8 Saturday

9 Sunday

Notes and shit

February 2025

10 Monday

11 Tuesday

12 Wednesday

Important as fuck

Fucking grateful for…

Be your own valentine. Break up with negative thoughts, bitch.

13 Thursday

14 Friday
Valentine's Day

15 Saturday

16 Sunday

Notes and shit

February 2025

17 Monday
Presidents' Day (US)

18 Tuesday

19 Wednesday

Important as fuck

Fucking grateful for…

You fucking rock. Please don't worry about assholes. I'll take care of them. xoxo Karma

20 Thursday

21 Friday

22 Saturday

23 Sunday

Notes and shit

February-March 2025

24 Monday

25 Tuesday

26 Wednesday

Important as fuck

Fucking grateful for…

What's your beauty secret? Drink water and glow like fucking sunshine?

27 Thursday

28 Friday
Ramadan begins

1 Saturday

2 Sunday

Notes and shit

March 2025

Sunday	Monday	Tuesday	Wednesday
February 2025 S M T W T F S 　　　　　　 1 2 3 4 5 6 7 8 9 10 11 12 13 14 15 16 17 18 19 20 21 22 23 24 25 26 27 28	**April 2025** S M T W T F S 　　 1 2 3 4 5 6 7 8 9 10 11 12 13 14 15 16 17 18 19 20 21 22 23 24 25 26 27 28 29 30		
2	3	4 Mardi Gras	5 Ash Wednesday
9 Daylight Saving Time begins (US, CA)	10	11	12
16	17 St. Patrick's Day	18	19
23	24	25	26
30 Mother's Day (UK), Eid al-Fitr begins	31		

Waking up and kicking ass again today? That's so you.

Thursday	Friday	Saturday	Important shit
		1	_____
6	7	8 International Women's Day	_____
13 Purim begins	14	15	_____
20 Spring begins (Northern Hemisphere)	21	22	_____
27	28	29	_____
			_____

March 2025

3 Monday

4 Tuesday
Mardi Gras

5 Wednesday
Ash Wednesday

Important as fuck

Fucking grateful for...

You will fuck up. We all do. And then you will rise up like a fucking phoenix. But maybe do something nice for yourself first. Grab a coffee or watch a show or something. Then do the phoenix-y thing.

6 Thursday

7 Friday

8 Saturday
International Women's Day

9 Sunday
Daylight Saving Time begins (US, CA)

Notes and shit

March 2025

10 Monday
11 Tuesday
12 Wednesday

Important as fuck

Fucking grateful for...

Choosing your happiness over someone else's fucking drama? Bold choice.

13 Thursday
Purim begins

14 Friday

15 Saturday

16 Sunday

Notes and shit

March 2025

17 Monday
St. Patrick's Day

18 Tuesday

19 Wednesday

Important as fuck

Fucking grateful for…

In honor of St. Patrick's Day, all "colorful" language will be green. F☘ck It!

20 Thursday
Spring begins (Northern Hemisphere)

21 Friday

22 Saturday

23 Sunday

Notes and shit

March 2025

24 Monday

25 Tuesday

26 Wednesday

Important as fuck

Fucking grateful for…

Don't take shit from anyone. Especially not yourself!

27 Thursday

28 Friday

29 Saturday

30 Sunday
Mother's Day (UK), Eid al-Fitr begins

Notes and shit

April 2025

Sunday	Monday	Tuesday	Wednesday
March 2025	*May 2025*	**1** April Fools' Day	**2**
6	**7**	**8**	**9**
13 Palm Sunday	**14**	**15** Tax Day (US)	**16**
20 Easter	**21** Easter Monday	**22** Earth Day	**23**
27	**28**	**29**	**30**

You express yourself beautifully. With your eyes, your smile, your words... and your middle finger.

Thursday	Friday	Saturday	Important shit
3	4	5	_____
10	11	12 Passover begins	_____
17	18 Good Friday	19	_____
24	25 Anzac Day (AU)	26	_____
			_____

March-April 2025

31 Monday

1 Tuesday
April Fools' Day

2 Wednesday

Important as fuck

Fucking grateful for…

You're amazing, beautiful, confident, delightful, empathetic, friendly, generous, happy, intelligent, joyful, kind ... Damn, describing you is easy. Doing it without swearing is the hard part!

3 Thursday

4 Friday

5 Saturday

6 Sunday

Notes and shit

April 2025

7 Monday

8 Tuesday

9 Wednesday

Important as fuck

Fucking grateful for...

You attract good shit and block bullshit as effortlessly as raising your middle finger

10 Thursday

11 Friday

12 Saturday
Passover begins

13 Sunday
Palm Sunday

Notes and shit

April 2025

14 Monday

15 Tuesday
Tax Day (US)

16 Wednesday

Important as fuck

Fucking grateful for...

Swearing is your love language

17 Thursday

18 Friday
Good Friday

19 Saturday

20 Sunday
Easter

Notes and shit

April 2025

21 Monday
Easter Monday

22 Tuesday
Earth Day

23 Wednesday

Important as fuck

Fucking grateful for…

You have a long year of kicking ass ahead of you. So, stay stretchy, bitch. You don't want to pull a muscle.

24 Thursday

25 Friday
Anzac Day (AU)

26 Saturday

27 Sunday

Notes and shit

May 2025

Sunday	Monday	Tuesday	Wednesday
APRIL 2025 S M T W T F S 　 　 1 2 3 4 5 6 7 8 9 10 11 12 13 14 15 16 17 18 19 20 21 22 23 24 25 26 27 28 29 30	**JUNE 2025** S M T W T F S 1 2 3 4 5 6 7 8 9 10 11 12 13 14 15 16 17 18 19 20 21 22 23 24 25 26 27 28 29 30		
4	5 Cinco de Mayo (US), Early May Bank Holiday (UK)	6	7
11 Mother's Day (US, CA, AU)	12	13	14
18	19 Victoria Day (CA)	20	21
25	26 Memorial Day (US), Spring Bank Holiday (UK)	27	28

Play like a girl, win like a fucking boss

Thursday	Friday	Saturday	Important shit
1	2	3	_____
8	9	10	_____
15	16	17 Armed Forces Day (US)	_____
22	23	24	_____
29	30	31	_____

April-May 2025

28 Monday

29 Tuesday

30 Wednesday

Important as fuck

Fucking grateful for…

Doubts can pile up like clutter. But at least you don't have to stress about what to get rid of. All that shit is TRASH.

1 Thursday

2 Friday

3 Saturday

4 Sunday

Notes and shit

May 2025

5 Monday
Cinco de Mayo (US), Early May Bank Holiday (UK)

6 Tuesday

7 Wednesday

Important as fuck

Fucking grateful for…

Asking for help is a sign of strength. Get your reps in, bitch.

8 Thursday

9 Friday

10 Saturday

11 Sunday
Mother's Day (US, CA, AU)

Notes and shit

May 2025

12 Monday

13 Tuesday

14 Wednesday

Important as fuck

Fucking grateful for…

Your opinions, like your heart, are fucking gold

15 Thursday

16 Friday

17 Saturday
Armed Forces Day (US)

18 Sunday

Notes and shit

May 2025

19 Monday
Victoria Day (CA)

20 Tuesday

21 Wednesday

Important as fuck

Fucking grateful for…

Want to master the art of saying "No"? Easy. Use bold, colorful language, like "Hell No," "Are you fucking kidding me?," and "Fuck off." And voila! You've got a masterpiece.

22 Thursday

23 Friday

24 Saturday

25 Sunday

Notes and shit

May-June 2025

26 Monday
Memorial Day (US), Spring Bank Holiday (UK)

27 Tuesday

28 Wednesday

Important as fuck

Fucking grateful for...

Say "Sayonara" to imposter syndrome, that toxic bitch

29 Thursday

30 Friday

31 Saturday

1 Sunday
Shavuot begins

Notes and shit

June 2025

Sunday	Monday	Tuesday	Wednesday
1 Shavuot begins	2	3	4
8	9	10	11
15 Father's Day (US, UK, CA)	16	17	18
22	23	24	25
29	30		

You float over fuckery like a badass butterfly

Thursday	Friday	Saturday	Important shit
5	6 Eid al-Adha begins	7	
12	13	14 Flag Day (US)	
19 Juneteenth (US)	20 Summer begins (Northern Hemisphere)	21 King's Birthday (UK), National Indigenous Peoples Day (CA)	
26 Muharram begins	27	28	

MAY 2025

S	M	T	W	T	F	S
				1	2	3
4	5	6	7	8	9	10
11	12	13	14	15	16	17
18	19	20	21	22	23	24
25	26	27	28	29	30	31

JULY 2025

S	M	T	W	T	F	S
		1	2	3	4	5
6	7	8	9	10	11	12
13	14	15	16	17	18	19
20	21	22	23	24	25	26
27	28	29	30	31		

June 2025

2 Monday

3 Tuesday

4 Wednesday

Important as fuck

Fucking grateful for…

Everything you need to succeed is within you. You're like a beautiful, walking, talking purse full of useful shit.

5 Thursday

6 Friday
Eid al-Adha begins

7 Saturday

8 Sunday

Notes and shit

June 2025

9 Monday

10 Tuesday

11 Wednesday

Important as fuck

Fucking grateful for…

You even brighten up Mondays, you awesome bitch

12 Thursday

13 Friday

14 Saturday
Flag Day (US)

15 Sunday
Father's Day (US, UK, CA)

Notes and shit

June 2025

16 Monday

17 Tuesday

18 Wednesday

Important as fuck

Fucking grateful for…

Being yourself is the best thing for you. But you're also setting a great example for aspiring bitches everywhere.

19 Thursday
Juneteenth (US)

20 Friday
Summer begins (Northern Hemisphere)

21 Saturday
King's Birthday (UK), National Indigenous Peoples Day (CA)

22 Sunday

Notes and shit

June 2025

23 Monday
24 Tuesday
25 Wednesday

Important as fuck

Fucking grateful for...

Keep your friends close and your enemies... can go fuck themselves

26 Thursday
Muharram begins

27 Friday

28 Saturday

29 Sunday

Notes and shit

July 2025

Sunday	Monday	Tuesday	Wednesday
JUNE 2025 S M T W T F S 1 2 3 4 5 6 7 8 9 10 11 12 13 14 15 16 17 18 19 20 21 22 23 24 25 26 27 28 29 30	AUGUST 2025 S M T W T F S 1 2 3 4 5 6 7 8 9 10 11 12 13 14 15 16 17 18 19 20 21 22 23 24 25 26 27 28 29 30 31	1 Canada Day (CA)	2
6	7	8	9
13	14	15	16
20	21	22	23
27	28	29	30

Rock what you got, you fabulous bitch

Thursday	Friday	Saturday	Important shit
3	4 Independence Day (US)	5	_____ _____ _____ _____ _____
10	11	12	_____ _____ _____ _____ _____
17	18	19	_____ _____ _____ _____ _____
24	25	26	_____ _____ _____ _____ _____
31			_____ _____ _____ _____

June-July 2025

30 Monday

1 Tuesday
Canada Day (CA)

2 Wednesday

Important as fuck

Fucking grateful for…

Overwhelmed? Chuck some shit in the fuck-it bucket. Perfection? Fuck it. What "they" say? Fuck it. Now you try it :)

3 Thursday

4 Friday
Independence Day (US)

5 Saturday

6 Sunday

Notes and shit

July 2025

7 Monday

8 Tuesday

9 Wednesday

Important as fuck

Fucking grateful for…

You do amazing things every fucking day. And some days, just getting out of bed will feel like an amazing accomplishment. Every win counts, bitch.

10 Thursday

11 Friday

12 Saturday

13 Sunday

Notes and shit

July 2025

14 Monday   15 Tuesday   16 Wednesday

Important as fuck

Fucking grateful for…

Plan for the day: Wake up. Spread fucking joy. Repeat.

17 Thursday

18 Friday

19 Saturday

20 Sunday

Notes and shit

July 2025

21 Monday22 Tuesday23 Wednesday

Important as fuckFucking grateful for…

look at you being talented, kind and beautiful. That's some badass multitasking, bitch.

24 Thursday

25 Friday

26 Saturday

27 Sunday

Notes and shit

July-August 2025

28 Monday

29 Tuesday

30 Wednesday

Important as fuck

Fucking grateful for…

Ignore haters who try to shit on your success. It's just their little hater thing. like some kind of stupid "crapbooking" hobby.

31 Thursday

1 Friday

2 Saturday

3 Sunday

Notes and shit

August 2025

Sunday	Monday	Tuesday	Wednesday
3	4 Civic Holiday (CA)	5	6
10	11	12	13
17	18	19	20
24	25 Summer Bank Holiday (UK)	26	27
31			

Your road to fucking happiness is paved with good intentions and even better actions

Thursday	Friday	Saturday	Important shit
	1	2	_____
7	8	9	_____
14	15	16	_____
21	22	23	_____
28	29	30	_____
			_____

August 2025

4 Monday
Civic Holiday (CA)

5 Tuesday

6 Wednesday

Important as fuck

Fucking grateful for…

You are a ray of fucking sunshine no matter how much shade assholes try to throw

7 Thursday

8 Friday

9 Saturday

10 Sunday

Notes and shit

August 2025

11 Monday

12 Tuesday

13 Wednesday

Important as fuck

Fucking grateful for...

You're too grounded to give a flying fuck

14 Thursday

15 Friday

16 Saturday

17 Sunday

Notes and shit

August 2025

18 Monday

19 Tuesday

20 Wednesday

Important as fuck

Fucking grateful for…

"Fuck No" is a perfectly acceptable way to say "No." So is, "Fuck Nope." Sounds weird, at first, but it's oddly satisfying. Try it ;)

21 Thursday

22 Friday

23 Saturday

24 Sunday

Notes and shit

August 2025

25 Monday
Summer Bank Holiday (UK)

26 Tuesday

27 Wednesday

Important as fuck

Fucking grateful for…

Your brain tries to crank up the volume on bad shit and mutes the good shit. Flip the switch on that bitch.

28 Thursday

29 Friday

30 Saturday

31 Sunday

Notes and shit

September 2025

Sunday	Monday	Tuesday	Wednesday
	1 Labor Day (US, CA)	2	3
7 Father's Day (AU)	8	9	10
14	15	16	17
21	22 Fall begins (Northern Hemisphere), Rosh Hashanah begins	23	24
28	29	30 National Day for Truth and Reconciliation (CA)	

Keep going, keep growing, keep knowing your fucking worth

Thursday	Friday	Saturday	Important shit
4	5	6	
11 Patriot Day (US)	12	13	
18	19	20	
25	26	27	

AUGUST 2025

S	M	T	W	T	F	S
					1	2
3	4	5	6	7	8	9
10	11	12	13	14	15	16
17	18	19	20	21	22	23
24	25	26	27	28	29	30
31						

OCTOBER 2025

S	M	T	W	T	F	S
			1	2	3	4
5	6	7	8	9	10	11
12	13	14	15	16	17	18
19	20	21	22	23	24	25
26	27	28	29	30	31	

September 2025

1 Monday
Labor Day (US, CA)

2 Tuesday

3 Wednesday

Important as fuck

Fucking grateful for…

You are smart, funny, and kind. And the best part is you can have a friendly chat with yourself any time you want, you lucky bitch

4 Thursday

5 Friday

6 Saturday

7 Sunday
Father's Day (AU)

Notes and shit

September 2025

8 Monday
9 Tuesday
10 Wednesday

Important as fuck

Fucking grateful for...

Use your powers for good. A little villainy is fine, but mostly good. Okay bitch?

11 Thursday
Patriot Day (US)

12 Friday

13 Saturday

14 Sunday

Notes and shit

September 2025

15 Monday

16 Tuesday

17 Wednesday

Important as fuck

Fucking grateful for...

You don't owe haters the time of day, much less your precious fucks

18 Thursday

19 Friday

20 Saturday

21 Sunday

Notes and shit

September 2025

22 Monday
Fall begins (Northern Hemisphere), Rosh Hashanah begins

23 Tuesday

24 Wednesday

Important as fuck

Fucking grateful for...

If you were any more magical, rainbows would shoot from your ass and glitter would fly from your mouth. Not sure we need that. So you're just the perfect amount of magical.

25 Thursday

26 Friday

27 Saturday

28 Sunday

Notes and shit

October 2025

Sunday	Monday	Tuesday	Wednesday
September 2025	*November 2025*		**1** Yom Kippur begins
5	**6** Sukkot begins	**7**	**8**
12	**13** Columbus Day (US), Indigenous Peoples' Day (US), Thanksgiving (CA)	**14**	**15**
19	**20** Diwali begins	**21**	**22**
26	**27**	**28**	**29**

You're so fucking awesome, it's scary

Thursday	Friday	Saturday	Important shit
2	3	4	_____
9	10	11	_____
16	17	18	_____
23	24	25	_____
30	31 Halloween		_____

September-October 2025

29 Monday

30 Tuesday
National Day of Truth and Reconciliation (CA)

1 Wednesday
Yom Kippur begins

Important as fuck

Fucking grateful for...

Pretend it's fun and get it done, bitch

2 Thursday

3 Friday

4 Saturday

5 Sunday

Notes and shit

October 2025

6 Monday
Sukkot begins

7 Tuesday

8 Wednesday

Important as fuck

Fucking grateful for…

Remember: You can love being cozy AF and still be a badass

9 Thursday

10 Friday

11 Saturday

12 Sunday

Notes and shit

October 2025

13 Monday
Columbus Day (US), Indigenous Peoples' Day (US), Thanksgiving Day (CA)

14 Tuesday

15 Wednesday

Important as fuck

Fucking grateful for…

If it feels like you're having far more negative thoughts than positive ones, it's because our brains are stuck in the fucking Stone Age. (Thanks, evolution, you slow fuck.) Keep looking on the bright side. Your brain will catch up!

16 Thursday

17 Friday

18 Saturday

19 Sunday

Notes and shit

October 2025

20 Monday
Diwali begins

21 Tuesday

22 Wednesday

Important as fuck

Fucking grateful for...

When you realize you don't have to be fucking perfect, you can be awesome

23 Thursday

24 Friday

25 Saturday

26 Sunday

Notes and shit

October-November 2025

27 Monday

28 Tuesday

29 Wednesday

Important as fuck

Fucking grateful for…

Treat yo' self, witch

30 Thursday

31 Friday
Halloween

1 Saturday

2 Sunday
Daylight Saving Time ends (US, CA)

Notes and shit

November 2025

Sunday	Monday	Tuesday	Wednesday
October 2025 S M T W T F S 　　　 1 2 3 4 5 6 7 8 9 10 11 12 13 14 15 16 17 18 19 20 21 22 23 24 25 26 27 28 29 30 31	**December 2025** S M T W T F S 　 1 2 3 4 5 6 7 8 9 10 11 12 13 14 15 16 17 18 19 20 21 22 23 24 25 26 27 28 29 30 31		
2 Daylight Saving Time ends (US, CA)	3	4 Election Day (US)	5
9	10	11 Veterans Day (US), Remembrance Day (UK, CA, AU)	12
16	17	18	19
23	24	25	26
30			

Today's plan: grateful heart, clear boundaries, strong fucking language

Thursday	Friday	Saturday	Important shit
		1	_____
6	7	8	_____
13	14	15	_____
20	21	22	_____
27 Thanksgiving Day (US)	28	29	_____
			_____

November 2025

3 Monday

4 Tuesday
Election Day (US)

5 Wednesday

Important as fuck

Fucking grateful for...

Cue your favorite hype music, let it rev you up, and launch this fucking day!

6 Thursday

7 Friday

8 Saturday

9 Sunday

Notes and shit

November 2025

10 Monday

11 Tuesday
Veterans Day (US), Remembrance Day (UK, CA, AU)

12 Wednesday

Important as fuck

Fucking grateful for…

Life can be tough as Hell, and it doesn't come with instructions. Not that you'd read them, you fucking rebel.

13 Thursday

14 Friday

15 Saturday

16 Sunday

Notes and shit

November 2025

17 Monday

18 Tuesday

19 Wednesday

Important as fuck

Fucking grateful for…

Fun fact: Swearing always helps

20 Thursday

21 Friday

22 Saturday

○
○
○

23 Sunday

○
○
○
○
○
○
○
○
○
○

○
○
○
○
○
○
○
○
○
○

○
○
○

Notes and shit

November 2025

24 Monday

25 Tuesday

26 Wednesday

Important as fuck

Fucking grateful for…

The first rule of Feast Club? Stretchy pants

27 Thursday
Thanksgiving Day (US)

28 Friday

29 Saturday

30 Sunday

Notes and shit

December 2025

Sunday	Monday	Tuesday	Wednesday
	1	2	3
7	8	9	10
14 Hanukkah begins	15	16	17
21 Winter begins (Northern Hemisphere)	22	23	24 Christmas Eve
28	29	30	31 New Year's Eve

Eat, drink and be sweary

Thursday	Friday	Saturday	Important shit
4	5	6	
11	12	13	
18	19	20	
25 Christmas Day	26 Boxing Day (UK, CA, AU), Kwanzaa begins	27	

NOVEMBER 2025

S	M	T	W	T	F	S
						1
2	3	4	5	6	7	8
9	10	11	12	13	14	15
16	17	18	19	20	21	22
23	24	25	26	27	28	29
30						

JANUARY 2026

S	M	T	W	T	F	S
				1	2	3
4	5	6	7	8	9	10
11	12	13	14	15	16	17
18	19	20	21	22	23	24
25	26	27	28	29	30	31

December 2025

1 Monday

2 Tuesday

3 Wednesday

- ○
- ○
- ○
- ○
- ○
- ○
- ○
- ○
- ○
- ○

- ○
- ○
- ○
- ○
- ○
- ○
- ○
- ○
- ○
- ○

- ○
- ○
- ○
- ○
- ○
- ○
- ○
- ○
- ○
- ○

Important as fuck

Fucking grateful for…

You are a fucking gift! You won't fit in a stocking, though, so keep shopping, bitch.

4 Thursday

5 Friday

6 Saturday

7 Sunday

Notes and shit

December 2025

8 Monday
9 Tuesday
10 Wednesday

Important as fuck

Fucking grateful for...

Sleigh, bitch, sleigh

11 Thursday

12 Friday

13 Saturday

14 Sunday
Hanukkah begins

Notes and shit

December 2025

15 Monday 16 Tuesday 17 Wednesday

Important as fuck

Fucking grateful for...

The Ghosts of Christmas Past, Present and Future agree: you are fucking awesome

18 Thursday

19 Friday

20 Saturday

21 Sunday
Winter begins (Northern Hemisphere)

Notes and shit

December 2025

22 Monday **23 Tuesday** **24 Wednesday**
Christmas Eve

Important as fuck

Fucking grateful for…

Congratulations on making the "Nice list" <u>and</u> the "Naughty list" again this year, you merry fucking badass

25 Thursday
Christmas Day

26 Friday
Boxing Day (UK, CA, AU), Kwanzaa begins

27 Saturday

28 Sunday

Notes and shit

December 2025-January 2026

29 Monday

30 Tuesday

31 Wednesday
New Year's Eve

Important as fuck

Fucking grateful for...

Cheers to fun that makes you laugh so hard, no sound comes out! (But a little pee might ;)

1 Thursday
New Year's Day

2 Friday

3 Saturday

4 Sunday

Notes and shit

My Brilliant Thoughts & Shit

My Brilliant Thoughts & Shit

My Brilliant Thoughts & Shit

My Brilliant Thoughts & Shit

My Brilliant Thoughts & Shit

🎁 Bonus Gifts 🎁

Hello Awesome! I hope these swear word gifts help you laugh and feel positive AF. These are high-quality PDF files that you can print at home or using a printing service. Feel free to share with friends!

What's Included

Floral Color Prints
48 Sweary affirmation cards (2.5 x 3.5 in.)

Floral Color Prints
48 Sweary wall art posters (8.5 x 11 in.)

Black and White Coloring Pages
48 Sweary quote designs (8.5 x 11 in.)

How to Access

Option 1

Scan this QR code with your device

You will see a "Download" button for instant access

—OR—

Option 2

Type this URL into your web browser:

sassyquotespress.com/2025gifts

You will see a "Download" button for instant access

—OR—

Option 3

Email me at
jen@sassyquotespress.com

I would love to hear from you! I can't promise "instant access," but I will respond ASAP!

©2024 Sassy Quotes Press. All rights reserved. Not for commercial use.

More from Sassy Quotes Press

Check out more of our hilarious swear word planners, coloring books and gratitude journals. Available on your local Amazon marketplace.

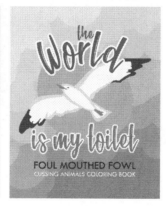
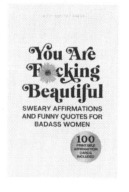

Want freebies and updates?

Sign up for free coloring pages and more at

SASSYQUOTESPRESS.COM

Questions? Comments? I would love to hear from you! Please email me at Jen@SassyQuotesPress.com

☆☆☆☆☆
A Favor Please!

Whether you purchased this book or received it as a gift...

Your star rating or review on Amazon makes a **HUGE** fucking difference to me as an independent publisher.

Seriously. I know your time is *valuable AF*. So, if you could take a quick minute to rate or review my book, I would be *very* grateful!

Two Quick Ways to Rate or Review on Amazon

ENTER IN YOUR WEB BROWSER → https://bit.ly/25swear

—OR—

SCAN WITH YOUR DEVICE →

Thank you! You are a fucking gem!

Made in the USA
Monee, IL
29 October 2024

68934535R00081